HOW

You Can Be a Fruitful Witness

BILL BRIGHT

NewLife
PUBLICATIONS

375 Highway 74 South, Suite A
Peachtree City, GA 30269

How You Can Be a Fruitful Witness

Published by
New*Life* Publications
A ministry of Campus Crusade for Christ
375 Highway 74 South, Suite A
Peachtree City, GA 30269

ISBN 1-56399-105-5

Design and typesetting by Genesis Publications.

Printed in the United States of America.

NewLife2000 is a registered service mark of Campus Crusade for Christ.

Unless otherwise indicated, Scripture quotations are taken from the *New International Version*, © 1973, 1978, 1984 by the International Bible Society. Published by Zondervan Bible Publishers, Grand Rapids, Michigan.

Scripture quotations designated TLB are from *The Living Bible*, © 1971 by Tyndale House Publishers, Wheaton, Illinois.

Scripture quotations designated NKJ are from the *New King James* version, © 1979, 1980, 1982 by Thomas Nelson Inc., Publishers, Nashville, Tennessee.

As a personal policy, Bill Bright has never accepted honorariums or royalties for his personal use. Any royalties from this book are dedicated to the glory of God and designated to the various ministries of Campus Crusade for Christ/*NewLife2000*.

What Is a Transferable Concept?

When our Lord commanded the eleven men with whom He had most shared His earthly ministry to go into all the world and make disciples of all nations, He told them to teach these new disciples all that He had taught them (Matthew 28:18–20).

Later the apostle Paul gave the same instructions to Timothy: "The things you have heard me say in the presence of many witnesses entrust to reliable men who will also be qualified to teach others" (2 Timothy 2:2).

In the process of counseling and interacting with tens of thousands of students, laymen, and pastors since 1951, our staff have discovered the following:

- Many church members (including people from churches that honor our Lord and faithfully teach His Word) are not sure of their salvation.
- The average Christian is living a defeated and frustrated life.
- The average Christian does not know how to share his faith effectively with others.

In our endeavor to help meet these three basic needs and to build Christian disciples, Campus Crusade for Christ has developed a series of "how to's"—or "transferable concepts"—in which we discuss many of the basic truths that Jesus and His disciples taught.

A "transferable concept" is an idea or a truth that can be transferred or communicated from one person to another and then to another, spiritual generation after generation, without distorting or diluting its original meaning.

As these basic truths—"transferable concepts"—of the Christian life are made available through the printed word, films, video tapes, and audio cassettes in every major language of the world, they could well be used of God to help transform the lives of tens of millions throughout the world.

We encourage you to master each of these concepts by reading it thoughtfully at least six times[1] until you are personally prepared to communicate it to others "who will also be qualified to teach others." By mastering these basic materials and discipling others to do the same, many millions of men and women can be reached and discipled for Christ and thus make a dramatic contribution toward the fulfillment of the Great Commission in our generation.

---

[1] Educational research confirms that the average person can master the content of a concept, such as this one, by reading it thoughtfully six times.

Contents

How You Can Be a Fruitful Witness

The Adventure of Witnessing

One of my responsibilities in giving leadership to Campus Crusade for Christ is to meet annually with the ministry directors of each continent.

In my travels to Asia and Europe, I visit with our staff and meet with thousands of pastors and laymen. On one occasion while meeting with a group of Christian leaders, I shared some of the highlights of the great worldwide spiritual harvest that is taking place today. One of the leaders interrupted me.

"I'm thrilled with your report," he said, "but I want to be very frank with you. I have not seen that kind of ministry myself. Why am I not having a more fruitful ministry?"

Perhaps you are asking yourself the same question. In the following pages, I want to share a biblical plan that will enable you to be fruitful in your witness for our Lord wherever you are and whatever the circumstances.

Before I share this plan with you, however, let me call to your attention the fifth chapter of Luke, which records an incident in the life of a seasoned fisherman—Simon Peter. He and his fellow workers had spent the entire night casting and gathering their nets but had not caught a single fish.

As these men were washing their nets, Jesus stepped into a boat and asked Peter to push out a little into the water so He could speak to the crowds that were pressing around Him.

When He had finished speaking, Jesus made a promise to this fisherman—a promise that I believe Peter, weary from his futile night of fishing, initially thought foolish. Jesus told Peter to go out a little further and let down his nets. If he did so, he would catch fish. Luke records Peter's response and what happened as a result:

"Sir," Simon [Peter] replied, "we worked hard all last night and didn't catch a thing. But if you say so, we'll try again." And this time their nets were so full that they began to tear! A shout for help brought their partners in the other boat and soon both boats were filled with fish and on the verge of sinking (Luke 5:5–7, TLB).

Jesus told these fishermen who were so awestruck with this demonstration of His power, "From now on you'll be fishing for the souls of men!" They were so overwhelmed with the presence and power of Jesus that they left their occupation to follow Him.

There is no experience in life more exciting and spiritually rewarding than the adventure of fishing for people. As you follow the Lord's instructions, your net too can be filled—even if you have never introduced anyone to Christ—even if you may be skeptical like Peter. But if you are also obedient like Peter, the Lord Jesus will honor you with the response of many people to your witness.

All over the world, I have asked two questions of millions of Christians—young and old, rich and poor, new believers and those who have known the Lord for more than half a century. I have asked these questions of some of the wealthiest and most famous Christians in the world. The answers are always the same no matter whom I ask.

1. *What is the most important experience of your life?*
   "Knowing Christ as my Savior is absolutely the most important experience in my life," is the inevitable answer.

2. *What is the most important thing that you can do to help
another person?*
Again, the answer is always the same: "Help him to know
Christ."

I am sure that, if you are a Christian, you would give the
same answers to these questions. Yet, how sad it is that so few
believers are sharing Christ with others. Obviously something
is wrong. If you are typical of the majority of Christians
today, you have never introduced anyone to Christ. You
would like to do so, however, and you know in your heart
that this is what God called you to do. Jesus calls to every
believer, "Follow me and I will make you fishers of men"
(Matthew 4:19).

When you begin to fill your nets with people whom you
introduce to Jesus Christ, you will begin the most exciting,
joyful, and rewarding adventure life has to offer. Perhaps,
like the disciples, you will leave the nets of your present
school, business, or other professional involvements to follow Him in this great adventure of witnessing for our Lord
in your Jerusalem, Judea, and Samaria and to the far corners
of the world.

The biblical plan that I want to share with you can be
divided into two categories: personal preparation and taking
the initiative.

Steps for Personal Preparation

*P*ersonal preparation is the key to becoming a fruitful Christian. If you follow these steps carefully
and prayerfully, they will transform your life and
witness for our dear Lord.

1. Be Sure That You Are a Christian

Millions of good, moral, religious people are active in the
church but are not sure of their present and eternal relationship with God. They are not sure they will go to heaven

when they die. In hundreds of our training conferences, which are attended by sincere and dedicated church members in each community, ten to twenty-five percent usually indicate that they either received Christ or gained the assurance of their salvation as a result of the training.

Let me give you an example. A remarkable young woman came to join our staff. My wife and I were much impressed with her and were confident that she would have a great ministry for our Lord. She came from a wonderful Christian family, and had attended Christian schools from kindergarten through college. She had been an active leader in church activities and was president of the Christian Women's Association in her area. She had even served as a counselor in several Billy Graham crusades. This dynamic young woman participated in all those activities you would expect of a radiant, fruitful Christian.

In speaking to the new staff during a training session, I stressed the importance of being sensitive to the needs of professing Christians who are not sure of their salvation. "Never assume that those who are unsure of their salvation are Christians, even if they have gone through the act of receiving Christ many times," I said. "You should not try to convince those who have doubts about their salvation that they are Christians. Rather, you should assume that they are not yet Christians, and you should prayerfully counsel them and lead them to the assurance of their salvation."

At the conclusion of my talk, this young woman said to me, "I don't think that I am a Christian, and I have always had doubts about my salvation."

Through the years, she had gone to various Christian leaders for spiritual counsel telling them that she was not sure she was a Christian. Since she believed all the basic doctrines of the faith, they assumed that she was a Christian and prayed and encouraged her. Although they prayed with her, she was never sure God heard her prayer. "There has been no evidence that Christ has come in," she said. "I am afraid I will die without Christ."

That day I had the privilege of sharing the good news of Ephesians 2:8,9 with this dear young woman who had been exposed to Christianity throughout her entire life. This time the Holy Spirit enabled her to trust God and His Word. By faith she received the Lord Jesus, the gracious gift of God's love, and her heart was filled with joy and praise and the assurance of her salvation. She was so excited that she called her parents, my wife, and others to tell them the good news that she now knew for sure that she would go to heaven when she dies.

One of my dearest friends during seminary days was the son of a famous evangelist. He came from a godly home. We met often for prayer. He memorized thousands of verses of Scripture and lived such a disciplined life for God that he was a constant challenge and inspiration to me. I was privileged to be the best man in his wedding.

He existed on a special diet of inexpensive food for days at a time, enabling him to live on twelve to fifteen cents a day, so that he could give more money to missions. He had finished his theological studies for his bachelor's degree and was studying for his doctorate in theology when he telephoned me one day to say, "Bill, I have just become a Christian."

I was amazed. "You're one of the best Christians I have ever known," I insisted. "I'm sure you have had an emotional experience of some kind."

"No," he said, "I have just become a Christian."

He then explained that all through the years, though he had never shared this, he had experienced conflict and uncertainty. Although he had invited Christ into his life numerous times, he had never before been sure that Jesus had actually come to be his Savior. Never before did he have the assurance of his salvation.

Perhaps you have never known the wonder, the joy, the assurance that Christ lives in you, that your sins are forgiven, and that you are a child of God. You may have believed in Christ intellectually for years. You may be active in the church; you may be very moral, religious, and godly in the eyes of your neighbors, and yet you have never experienced this new birth.

Becoming a Christian involves commitment of the total person, which can best be illustrated by the marriage relationship. Many years ago, for example, I became aware of a beautiful young woman whom I thought was the most wonderful girl in the world. As we became better acquainted, we fell in love and were married. But we were not married just because we were intellectually involved and admired each other, or because we were emotionally involved and loved each other. It was by an act of our wills by faith that we committed ourselves to each other as we stood one day before a minister and became husband and wife. In that moment, because of two words, "I do," we became legally married.

As a result, she left her home, and I left my home, and we started a third home. Now, there was no emotion when I said, "I do." The walls didn't shake, nor did lightning flash. As a matter of fact, I felt a little numb. But, we were no less married just because I didn't at that moment feel like shouting for joy. Those two words that expressed the desire of our hearts consummated our long engagement of three years. My love for Vonette has grown through the years, and I have told her thousands of times since that memorable marriage ceremony that I love her. But I have not proposed to her one single time since we said, "I do."

So it is in your relationship with Christ. Commitment to Christ involves your entire person—your intellect, your emotions, your will. It is not enough to believe intellectually that Jesus Christ is the Son of God; not enough to know that He died on the cross for your sins and was raised from the dead; not enough to be baptized, to be active in the church, and to read your Bible and pray daily. You do not become a Christian until by faith, as an act of your will, you receive the gift of God's grace—His love and forgiveness through the Lord Jesus Christ. When you receive Him by faith, you receive a new nature—you are born into God's family, and you begin to experience the reality of eternal life.

If you have never yet said to Christ, "I do receive You as my Savior from sin and as the Lord of my life," I encourage you to do so right now. Jesus said, "Here I am! I stand at the door and knock. If anyone hears my voice and opens the door, I will come in…" (Revelation 3:20).

Ask Him to come into your life. Then, on the authority of His promise, thank Him that He has come in as He promised to do. He will not lie to you.

After you have received Him, never insult Him by asking Him into your life again. The rest of your life, begin each day by thanking Him that He is in your life. He has promised to be with you always (Matthew 28:20), and He said, "Never will I leave you; never will I forsake you" (Deuteronomy 31:6; Hebrews 13:5).

I gave this message about faith at one of our city-wide Lay Institutes for Evangelism. At the conclusion of my message, a woman who had reached her twilight years came to me in tears. She said that she had been a Sunday school teacher for four decades.

"Seldom a day has passed during the last forty years that I haven't asked Christ into my life," she said. "But I was never sure that he was there. After tonight and for the rest of my life, I am going to say, "Thank You, Lord, that You are in my heart. I am never going to insult You again by asking You to come into my life, for now I am sure that You are already there."

Will you do the same? If you have never done so, do it now. Pause for a moment and, if the following prayer expresses the desire of your heart, make it your prayer:

Lord Jesus, I need You. I open the door of my life and receive You as my Savior and Lord.

Thank You for forgiving my sins. Take control of the throne of my life. Make me the kind of person You want me to be.

Thank You for coming into my life. The rest of my life I will thank You that You are in my life and will never leave me. Thank You that I now have eternal life as You promised.

2. Be Sure There Is No Unconfessed Sin in Your Life

If some sinful attitude or action is hindering your fellowship with God, He cannot live and love through you, and you will not be a joyful Christian or a fruitful witness for Christ.

According to Hebrews 10, Christ came as God's sacrifice for your sins. The Old Testament records that the Israelites took their animal sacrifice to the priest where it was slain and the blood was sprinkled on the altar as a covering for their sins. Then in the fullness of God's time and purpose, foretold by the prophets of the Old Testament, Jesus Christ, the Messiah, came to die for you. He came as God's sacrifice to shed His blood on the cross for your sins. As a result there is no further need of a sacrifice to be made for your sins.

You can add nothing to the assurance of salvation and eternal life that Christ accomplished for you on the cross. Tears and self-imposed disciplines do not add anything to His complete and perfect substitutionary sacrifice that He made for you on the cross. The only thing you can do to make Christ's death on the cross meaningful in your life is to confess your sins and accept His sacrifice as the full and final payment for all of your sins—past, present, and future. The

Bible, God's holy, inspired Word, says, "If we confess our sins, he is faithful and just and will forgive us our sins and purify us from all unrighteousness" (1 John 1:9).

In Greek, the original language of the New Testament, the word "confess" (*homologeo*) means to "agree with" or to "say along with." What do you do when you agree with God?

First, you acknowledge that the sin you have committed is wrong. God is holy; no sin can enter His presence. And yet God, who hates sin, loves the sinner. He loves you no matter what you do, but He hates your sin. When the Spirit of God says to you in that still, small voice, "I am grieved with your conduct, your attitude," you know what you have done is wrong, and you acknowledge—agree with God—that it is wrong.

Second, you acknowledge that all of your sins were paid for by Jesus when He shed His blood on the cross for you according to Hebrews 10. Now, thank Christ for dying for your sins.

Third, you repent. The original meaning of the word "repent" is literally "to have a change of mind." You change your attitude toward your sin, which of course—through the enabling power of the Holy Spirit—will result in a change of your actions. You willingly turn from doing what displeases God and begin doing what pleases Him.

You cannot live a holy life and grieve God's Holy Spirit at the same time! Failure to acknowledge your sin will result in divine discipline. Because God loves His children, He chastens, corrects, and disciplines those who are disobedient (Revelation 3:19). David records, "I cried to him [the Lord] for help...He would not have listened if I had not confessed my sins" (Psalm 66:17,18, TLB).

The minute the Spirit of God puts His finger on your sin, confess it. Breathe spiritually—exhale by confessing your sin. Whenever the Holy Spirit makes you aware of sin that you have committed or are committing, be quick to confess it. Confession of sin is essential for a holy life and a contagious, fruitful witness for our Lord.

3. Be Filled With the Spirit

One of my dear friends, who is a great Christian scholar, confessed to a group of fellow believers in one of our Lay Institutes for Evangelism that he was not a happy, joyful Christian and he seldom witnessed for Christ. Later I shared with him some of the truths about how to witness in the power of the Spirit. God touched his life. After an afternoon of sharing Christ, he came back that evening bubbling over with joy. He could hardly wait to tell us what God had done in his life. He shared how he had talked to two young college students about Christ, and in the process Christ had become more real to him than he had ever experienced.

Perhaps you spend hours in prayer and Bible study every day, but you are not joyful. You are not living that abundant life that Jesus promised.

In order to be fruitful in your witness for Christ, you must appropriate by faith the fullness of God's Spirit. Jesus promised, "You will receive power when the Holy Spirit comes on you; and you will be my witnesses in Jerusalem, and in all Judea and Samaria, and to the ends of the earth" (Acts 1:8).

Being filled with the Spirit involves inviting the Holy Spirit by faith to control and empower you—to enable you to live a holy, godly life and to make you a fruitful witness for Him. Two words and two verses are vital here:

First, remember the word *command*. Ephesians 5:18 says:

> *Do not get drunk on wine, which leads to debauchery.*
> *Instead, be filled with the Spirit.*

This means you are to be controlled and empowered by the Holy Spirit as a way of life. It is a command for every believer—not for the evangelist or pastor only, not just for the Sunday school teacher and other Christian leaders, but for everyone who believes in Jesus Christ.

Now relate God's *command* to His *promise*, found in 1 John 5:14,15:

> *This is the confidence we have in approaching God: that if we ask anything according to his will, he hears us. And if we know that he hears us—whatever we ask—we know that we have what we asked of him.*

On the basis of God's *command* and His *promise*, if you are willing to surrender the direction and control of your life to our Lord Jesus Christ, you can know that He will fill you when you by faith, as an act of your will, appropriate the fullness of His Holy Spirit.

Don't make the mistake of thinking that you must experience some great emotion. In fact, emotions can be very dangerous. Pour a gallon of gasoline on the ground, strike a match, and it goes up in flame and smoke—then it's all gone. Dramatic, but wasted.

Many people are so involved in emotions and in seeking experiences that they actually insult God. The Bible says, "The righteous will live by faith" (Romans 1:17), and "Everything that does not come from faith is sin" (Romans 14:23). The very act of seeking an emotional experience repudiates the concept of faith.

Many times when I stand in the pulpit or talk to individuals personally, I do not feel any great surge of spiritual power or emotion. Sometimes, because of much travel, speaking, and inadequate rest, my body is weary and my mind is dulled by fatigue. Yet—if there is no unconfessed sin in my life, and by faith I claim God's fullness—I know that I am filled with the Spirit even if I do not feel like it. I don't depend on feelings. I depend on God's Word—His command and His promise.

By faith you can know that you are filled with the Spirit constantly and continually the rest of your life as you con-

tinue to "breathe spiritually"—exhaling as you confess your sins, and inhaling as you appropriate God's power by faith.

Being filled with the Holy Spirit equips you for service as a witness for Christ. We say to our staff (who are now serving Christ in 155 major countries of the world, representing 98 percent of the world's population), "Don't go to your assignments unless you know beyond a shadow of a doubt that you are filled with the Holy Spirit." Only service performed for Christ in the power of the Holy Spirit is pleasing to God. Service performed for Him in the energy of the flesh is time wasted and dishonors His name, producing spiritual wood, hay, and straw that will be burned up on Christ's judgment day.

If at this moment you know that you are not filled with the Holy Spirit and you truly desire to be a man or woman of God, you can pray this prayer right now:

Lord Jesus, I truly desire to be a godly person. I turn from my sinful ways. I surrender the control of my life to You. I hold nothing back. I want You to be my Master and my Lord.

Now, on the authority of Your command *to be filled and Your* promise *that if we ask anything according to your will You will hear and answer us, by faith I receive the fullness of the Holy Spirit.*

If you prayed this prayer in faith, you can know on the basis of His *command* and on the authority of His *promise* that you are filled with the Holy Spirit right now! You can know this by faith—with or without emotions—simply by trusting God and His Word.

However, according to the promise of Jesus, "The one who obeys me is the one who loves me; and because he loves me, my Father will love him; and I will too, and I will reveal myself to him" (John 14:21, TLB). Since Jesus promised to manifest Himself to all who obey Him, proper emotions result when you live by faith and when you share your faith in Christ with others in the power of the Holy Spirit.

4. Be Prepared to Communicate Your Faith in Christ

Keeping Christ on the throne of your life as the Lord of your heart is the best preparation for communicating your faith. First Peter 3:15,16 says:

> *In your hearts set apart Christ as Lord. Always be prepared to…give the reason for the hope that you have. But do this with gentleness and respect, keeping a clear conscience, so that those who speak maliciously against your good behavior in Christ may be ashamed of their slander.*

Like any other skill, the ability to give the reason for the hope you have in Christ—or "witnessing"—can be done better after instruction and practice.

Let me illustrate. A pastor told me that he had been in Christian work for more than twenty-five years, but had never introduced anyone to Christ until after he had participated in one of our training conferences. He said, "Your message on how to witness in the Spirit and how to present the gospel through the use of the *Four Spiritual Laws* has changed my life. Never have I been so happy. Now I know something of the abundant life that Jesus promised!"

This Christian leader was beaming with newfound joy as he shared how he had, for the first time in his life, introduced not one person, but two people to our Savior.

During that same week of training, hundreds of students and the few laypeople in attendance had been used by God to pray personally with more than nine hundred people who received Christ through their witness. Training made the difference.

I thank God for the way He is using theological seminaries, Bible schools, and similar instructional Christian institutions, but you don't need long years of training before God can use you. Not everyone has the gift of evangelism, but every believer is called to "do the work of an evangelist" (2 Timothy 4:5). You have the privilege and responsibility of being a witness for your wonderful Lord Jesus. Christ's Great Commission recorded in Matthew 28:18–20 is for you.

By learning how to use a simple tool like the *Four Spiritual Laws* in the power of the Holy Spirit, you too can experience effectiveness in your witness.

Some Christians will be more fruitful than others. Don't be distressed if you find that some of your friends are introducing more people to Christ than you are. Just rest in the knowledge that those who come to Christ through the witness of a Christian are coming as a result of the ministry of the Spirit of God who alone enables you to bear fruit. Remember, *success in witnessing is simply taking the initiative to share Christ in the power of the Holy Spirit and leaving the results to God.*

I am personally convinced that if you give ten *Four Spiritual Laws* to non-Christians each day, at least one to five will receive Christ, depending on the country or culture.

Taking the Initiative

*P*ersonal preparation—being sure you are a Christian, confessing your sins, being filled with the Holy Spirit, and being prepared to communicate your faith in Christ—is the first part of how you can be a fruitful witness. The second is taking the initiative.

Four steps are involved in taking the initiative. Let's look at each briefly.

1. Pray

According to God's holy Word, if you ask anything in harmony with His will, He hears and answers you (1 John 5:14,15). Do you want your loved ones, friends, and neighbors to come to Christ? Begin to claim them for God.

Follow the example of our Lord, whose priestly prayer is recorded in John 17:20: "My prayer is not for them alone. I pray also for those who will believe in me through their message." Paul and the other writers of the New Testament were frequently requesting prayer for others as well as for themselves.

I have prayed for loved ones with whom I used to weep as I pleaded with them to come to Christ. Then one day I realized that God was not willing for them to perish—He loved them more than I did—and so I began to thank God in faith that they would become Christians. Most of them have already received Christ. But more names continue to be added to that list.

Just as Jesus prayed that the Holy Spirit would do a work in the lives of His disciples, so you can pray that the Holy Spirit would convict nonbelievers and give them a strong desire for the ways of God. The Scripture promises:

The Lord is not slow in keeping his promise, as some understand slowness. He is patient with you, not wanting anyone to perish, but everyone to come to repentance (2 Peter 3:9).

Sometimes, however, in His mysterious, sovereign timing, He chooses to wait for the prayers of a concerned believer to unleash the Holy Spirit in that person's heart. As someone has said, "Prayer is not conquering God's reluctance—but laying hold of God's willingness."

Although God is not willing for "anyone to perish, but everyone to come to repentance," His schedule is not always the same as yours. Continue to trust and thank Him for the salvation and spiritual growth of those for whom He has

impressed you to pray. From my personal experience and study of God's Word, I can assure you that the starting point in bringing a loved one to Christ is prayer.

Make a prayer list or keep a prayer diary and pray for specific non-Christians and Christians by name and for specific events. As God answers, record the date and describe how God has answered your prayers. In a short time you will have a record of God's faithfulness that will encourage and strengthen your faith and the faith of others.

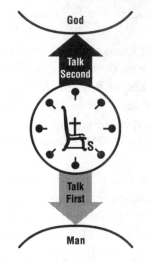

2. Go

One of the greatest barriers in witnessing is the problem of getting going. You hear all kinds of excuses: "I'm too busy," or "I'm waiting for the Holy Spirit to lead someone to me." Our Lord Jesus Christ has already commanded you to go tell the good news to all who will listen. Don't wait for them to come to you. As you follow Jesus, He will lead you to people whom He has prepared.

Remember, the greatest thing that has ever happened to you is knowing Christ, and the greatest thing that you can do for another is help him to know Christ. If this is true, you should begin to rethink your priorities. How are you spending your time? Are you taking time every day to share Christ with someone?

You may be encouraged to know that many on the staff of Campus Crusade for Christ, like myself, are by nature shy. We do not always find it easy to talk to others about Christ. But since Jesus came to seek and to save the lost and since He lives within us, we simply ask Him to give us the courage to speak powerfully for Him.

Whenever I am alone with a person for a few minutes, I assume that I am there by divine appointment to share the good news of God's love and forgiveness.

For instance, while in Atlanta I stopped at a shopping mall to purchase a tie. The store manager offered his services, and while choosing a tie to match the suit I was wearing, I told him I was in town to meet with a number of Christian leaders to talk about ways to bring our nation back to God. Then I asked, "Are you a Christian?"

He said he was not, but that he had considered becoming one. I showed him the *Four Spiritual Laws* booklet. As I read through the booklet, I came to Law Four, which explains how to receive Christ and ends with this prayer:

Lord Jesus, I need You. Thank You for dying on the cross for my sins. I open the door of my life and receive You as my Savior and Lord. Thank You for forgiving my sins and giving me eternal life. Take control of the throne of my life. Make me the kind of person You want me to be.

I asked, "Does this prayer express the desire of your heart?"

He stated that it did, so I suggested that he pray it aloud, which he did. And as soon as he finished, I prayed for him.

Then I asked him if he knew where Christ was in relation to him. He assured me that Christ was now in his life. I went on to explain how, according to God's Word, he not only could have assurance of eternal life, but could grow as a Christian.

As is my practice, I obtained his address to send important follow-up material.

Wherever I go, across America and in other countries, on planes, in restaurants, on elevators, in lecture halls, on the college campus, or among laymen, I meet people who are eager to receive Christ.

Sharing Christ with others should be a way of life for every Christian. When you awaken each morning, thank the Lord Jesus for living within you and ask Him to use your lips to speak of His love and forgiveness at every opportunity throughout the day.

3. Talk About Jesus

Paul said, "Everywhere we go we talk about Christ to all who will listen" (Colossians 1:28, TLB). Don't just talk about peripheral matters, such as the weather, sports, government, and business. Pray and expect God to enable you to introduce His Son into the conversation.

A quiet, loving widow in her early thirties has led dozens of her relatives, friends, and neighbors to the Lord Jesus. Nearly every Sunday she brings someone new to church with her. Many of these she has introduced to Christ during the previous week.

Once she was asked, "How do you manage to share your faith with so many people?"

She answered, "I ask myself, 'If I don't tell them about the Lord Jesus, who will?' And I don't have a good answer for that."

Today, an ever-increasing number of Christians are constantly being used by God to introduce others to our Savior because they have been trained to talk about Christ in the power of the Holy Spirit. They do not get sidetracked to discuss nonessential matters. That's the reason the *Four Spiritual Laws* booklet is so effective—it keeps the conversation centered on the person of Christ, away from distracting issues

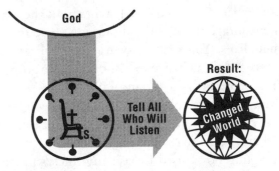

that direct attention away from our Lord. And it makes your presentation of the gospel simple and understandable.

Many people express antagonism toward God and want nothing to do with religion. But when you tell them about Jesus, they respond.

I recall a taxi driver in Australia who said to me, "I gave up all religion in World War II. I want nothing to do with a God who allows people to kill each other."

"Wait a minute," I said. "You are accusing God of something for which man is responsible. It is the evil in man, his sin, that causes him to hate and steal and kill."

I explained the difference between religion, which is man's search for God, and Christianity, which is God's revelation of Himself in Christ to man. As I talked to him about the person of Christ, this man's entire attitude changed. Soon he said that he would like to pray with me and receive Christ.

Many people today are also antagonistic toward the organized church in general, and if you are going to reach them for the Savior, you must talk first about the Savior, not about the church. After they receive Christ, most of them will want to become active in the church.

Others are antagonistic toward the Bible as the Word of God. You do not have to prove the Bible—just use it. Use it even with people who say they do not believe it. God has promised that His Word will accomplish His purposes (Isaiah 55:11).

If you expect God to use you, talk about the Savior—and always encourage those with whom you share to invite Him into their lives. You really haven't "evangelized" until you have given people a chance to respond to the gospel by inviting Christ to be their Savior and Lord.

As you talk to people about the Savior, you will discover that many are ready to receive Him the very first time you talk to them. Some may need to "ripen" a bit.

As a young boy I used to visit my uncle's peach orchard. We would always pick the ripe peaches, but leave the green ones. Two days later, we would return to the same tree and pick more ripe peaches. Every two days we would pick yet more ripe ones. So it is in our witness for Christ. Be prayerfully sensitive to people and their readiness for the gospel. Ripe for harvest, some will readily receive Christ; others, like green fruit, will not be ready.

Do not argue with those who are not ready. Do not insult them; do not browbeat them or try to pressure them into "making a decision for Christ." Give them something appropriate to read (like the *Four Spiritual Laws* or *A Man Without Equal*), leave them with a prayer, talk to them later—as the Lord gives opportunity—but continue to look for those who are ripe for harvest. They are all around you. Thousands, even millions, of people whose hearts have already been prepared by the Holy Spirit are waiting to receive Christ.

On one plane trip, for example, I talked to two people who were "spiritually ripe." One was an eighty-year-old woman who received Christ as her Savior. The other, the president of a large corporation, had always believed that Jesus Christ was the Son of God and had died for his sins, but had been too busy with other things to make a commitment to Christ personally.

On the same trip, at Cornell University where I addressed students and faculty, the president of a sizable business approached me. He was visiting his son who was a new Christian of six months.

"I want to thank you for helping my son spiritually," he said.

Then I asked if he had ever received Christ. He replied that he had not, but that he wanted to. We bowed in prayer and, to his son's great joy, he committed his life to our Savior.

Take the initiative by praying, by going to others, by talking about Jesus, and finally, by expecting God to use you.

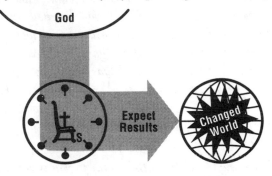

4. Expect God to Use You

When you talk about Jesus, expect men and women to respond—not on the basis of positive thinking, but because of God's faithfulness, His love, His sovereignty, His power, and His promise that He is not willing that any should perish, but that all should come to repentance.

The Lord Jesus promised His supernatural resources to all who join with Him in helping to fulfill the Great Commission. He told His disciples:

"I have been given all authority in heaven and earth. Therefore go and make disciples in all the nations, baptizing them in the name of the Father and of the Son and of the Holy Spirit, and then teach these new disciples to obey all the commands I have given you; and be sure of this—that I am with you always, even to the end of the world" (Matthew 28:18–20, TLB).

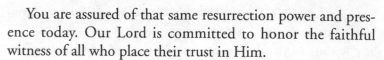

You are assured of that same resurrection power and presence today. Our Lord is committed to honor the faithful witness of all who place their trust in Him.

It is interesting to note that while the disciples met with strong and often bitter opposition, the Christian movement experienced phenomenal growth. The gospel has the power to change people's lives, as was expressed in Paul's letters to the churches in Thessalonica and Colosse:

> *When we brought you the Good News, it was not just meaningless chatter to you; no, you listened with great interest. What we told you produced a powerful effect upon you, for the Holy Spirit gave you great and full assurance that what we said was true. And you know how our very lives were further proof to you of the truth of our message. So you became our followers and the Lord's; for you received our message with joy from the Holy Spirit"* (1 Thessalonians 1:5,6, TLB).

> *The same Good News that came to you is going out all over the world and changing lives everywhere, just as it changed yours that very first day you heard it and understood about God's great kindness to sinners"* (Colossians 1:6, TLB).

One of the greatest lies of the centuries is the attitude among Christians that people do not want to know God personally. Because of this, many Christians approach others with a negative attitude as if to say, "You don't want to become a Christian, do you?" By their negative attitude, they inhibit others from expressing their need for Christ. Let me encourage you to expect that God has already prepared the hearts of those who are eager to receive Christ, and you will find that He really has.

After more than forty-five years of sharing Christ with millions of students and laymen, individually and in small and large groups, I can tell you that the Holy Spirit has created a hunger for God in the hearts of multitudes around the world. Millions are waiting for someone to tell them about our wonderful Savior, ready to receive Him as their very own.

For example, at one of our pastors' conferences in Haiti, more than 1,000 people received Christ as 550 pastors and lay preachers prayed with them, one and two at a time, during four hours of witnessing.

At Daytona Beach, during an Easter vacation, approximately 1,500 Campus Crusade staff members and university students introduced more than 3,500 students to Christ through their witness.

In Southern California, a similar number of trainees introduced approximately 2,000 university students to Christ in one day of witnessing at the beach.

Most of our staff, lay, and student volunteers report that ten to seventy-five percent of the people to whom they make a clear presentation of the gospel receive Christ. The percentage of response often depends on the country and culture. Yet, we find that the Spirit of God has prepared the hearts of multitudes of men and women to respond to Christ. As Jesus said, "Open your eyes and look at the fields! They are ripe for harvest" (John 4:35). Not everyone with whom you share Christ will receive Him, but God will use you to both sow and harvest in His kingdom as you trust Him.

Success in Witnessing

*E*xpect results when you witness for Christ. But remember, however God chooses to use your faithfulness in witnessing, your responsibility is to present Christ. It is His responsibility to draw people to Himself. As I have said earlier, *success in witnessing is simply taking the initiative to share Christ in the power of the Holy Spirit and leaving the results to God.*

In these pages I have presented a biblical plan that will enable you to be successful in reaching others for Christ. First you must begin by preparing yourself:

1. Be sure you are a Christian.

2. Be sure there is no unconfessed sin in your life.

3. Be filled with the Spirit.

4. Be prepared to communicate your faith in Christ.

Then, you must take the initiative by:

1. Praying.

2. Going to others.

3. Talking about the Lord Jesus.

4. Expecting God to use you.

Following this plan consistently will enable you to be fruitful for God as a way of life. No other experience in this world can compare to that of witnessing for Christ in the power of the Holy Spirit. Will you join me in this adventure?

NOTE

Remember, *How You Can Be a Fruitful Witness* is a transferable concept. You can master it by reading it six times; then pass it on to others as our Lord commands us in Matthew 28:20, "Teach these new disciples to obey all the commands I have given you" (TLB). he apostle Paul encouraged us to do the same: "The things you have heard me say in the presence of many witnesses entrust to reliable men who will also be qualified to teach others" (2 Timothy 2:2).

Self-Study Guide

1. What do these verses say about feelings as related to living the Christian life?

   a. John 14:23

   b. Romans 14:21,23

   c. Galatians 3:11

2. Do you have a list of nonbelievers for whom you pray? Will you claim God's promise to answer by pledging with Him to pray for others daily?

3. In what sense is sharing the gospel a demonstration of your love for others?

4. What are some things that may keep you from talking to others about Jesus? (See page 22.)

5. Why is it important for you to take the initiative to share Christ instead of waiting for nonbelievers to come to you? (See page 23.)

6. Why is it essential to first talk about Jesus rather than other issues (such as joining a church, apologetics, and so on)? (See pages 25,26.)

7. What does God say about His Word? How does this affect your view of evangelism?

   a. Isaiah 55:11

   b. Ephesians 1:13

   c. Colossians 1:5,6

   d. Hebrews 4:12

8. What does John 4:35 mean? How does it apply to you?

9. What is one essential ingredient needed to please Christ? (See Hebrews 11:6.)

10. Each of us has moments when we don't feel like sharing our faith. Identify your feelings—fear, inadequacy, self-consciousness, and so on—that often keep you from witnessing. What steps will you take in the coming week to overcome these feelings?

11. What does it mean to "expect results from God" as you witness? What are the consequences of not expecting results? (See pages 27–29.)

12. List five people you know who have not received Christ as their Savior and Lord. What steps will you take this week to introduce them to Jesus Christ?

Group Discussion Questions

1. Share briefly how you personally received the assurance that Christ had come into your life. What steps led to your trusting Christ? How could this be helpful in sharing Christ with others?

2. List and discuss Scripture verses that you think are especially helpful in giving a person assurance of his salvation.

3. Discuss the relationship between a consistent daily prayer life and a sensitivity to the convicting work of the Holy Spirit.

4. Find examples in the Book of Acts where the early Christians were filled with the Spirit. How did their subsequent actions demonstrate joy? What was the impact on their witness?

5. People today face tight schedules with limited amounts of time. With your group, think of creative ways that a Christian can maximize his time to give witnessing for Christ top priority.

6. You have heard the statement, "Success in witnessing is simply taking the initiative to share Christ in the power of the Holy Spirit and leaving the results to God." Share with your group how this statement can be a source of encouragement to you. If you talk to someone in the power of the Holy Spirit and that person does not receive Christ, why should you call that "successful witnessing"?

7. When you are witnessing, why is it important to talk about Jesus Christ? Does this mean that you are never to talk about politics, the church, business, or other things when you are telling others about Christ? (See Romans 10:9,14; John 1:12.)

8. Why is faith on your part important in bringing others to Christ? Discuss how your faith works in the lives of the

people to whom you witness. How do you use faith to fight against your spiritual enemies? (See Ephesians 6:10–20; Hebrews 11:6.)

9. Is there any one country, people group, or segment of society for which God has especially burdened you? Share this with your group. In addition to praying faithfully, what are some other steps you can take to reach these people for Christ? Discuss a strategy for reaching these goals.

How to Share Christ With Others

A well-known Christian leader, highly gifted as a theologian, shared with me his frustration over his lack of effectiveness and fruitfulness in witnessing for Christ.

I asked him, "What do you say when you seek to introduce a person to Christ?"

He explained his presentation, which was long and complicated. The large number of Bible verses he used would confuse most people and prevent them from making an intelligent decision.

I challenged him to use the *Four Spiritual Laws* presentation daily for the next thirty days and inform me of his experiences at the end of that time.

When I saw him two weeks later, he was overflowing with joy and excitement. "By simply reading the booklet to others," he said, "I have seen more people come to Christ during the last two weeks than I had previously seen in many months. It's hard to believe!"

The *Four Spiritual Laws* booklet presents a clear and simple explanation of the gospel of our Lord Jesus Christ.

This booklet, available in all major languages of the world, has been developed as a result of more than forty years of experience in counseling with thousands of college students on campuses in almost every country on every continent in the world, as well as with a comparable number of laymen, pastors, and high school students. It represents one way to share your faith effectively.

Benefits of the Four Laws

Using a tool such as the *Four Spiritual Laws* booklet offers many benefits. Let me list some of them:

• It helps you open your conversation easily and naturally.

- It begins with a positive statement: "God loves you and has a wonderful plan for your life."
- It presents the gospel and the claims of Christ clearly and simply.
- It gives you confidence because you know what you are going to say and how you are going to say it.
- It enables you to be prepared at all times and to stick to the subject without getting off on tangents.
- It makes it possible for you to be brief and to the point.
- It enables you to lead others to a personal decision through a suggested prayer.
- It offers suggestions for growth, and emphasizes the importance of involvement in the church.
- Of special importance, it is a "transferable tool" to give to those whom you introduce to Christ so that they can be encouraged and trained to lead others to Christ also. Paul exhorted Timothy, his young son in the faith:

   The things you have heard me say in the presence of many witnesses entrust to reliable men who will also be qualified to teach others (2 Timothy 2:2).

The *Four Spiritual Laws* enables those who receive Christ to go immediately to friends and loved ones and tell them of their newfound faith in Christ. It also enables them to show their friends and loved ones how they, too, can make a commitment to Christ.

Various Approaches

After a cordial, friendly greeting, you can use one of the following approaches to introduce the *Four Spiritual Laws* to a nonbeliever:

- "I'm reading a little booklet that really makes sense to a lot of people. I'd like to share it with you. Have you heard of the *Four Spiritual Laws?*"

- "Do you ever think about spiritual things?" (Pause for an answer.) "Have you ever heard of the *Four Spiritual Laws?*"
- "A friend of mine recently gave me this little booklet that really makes sense to me. I would like to share it with you. Have you ever heard of the *Four Spiritual Laws?*"
- "The content of this booklet has been used to change the lives of millions of people. It contains truths that I believe will be of great interest to you. Would you read it and give me your impression?"
- "It is believed that this little booklet is the most widely printed piece of literature in the world apart from the Bible.[2] Would you be interested in reading it?"

Here is a direct approach that you can use when you have only a few moments with an individual:

"If you died today, do you know for sure that you will go to heaven?"

If the answer is yes, ask:

"On what do you base that knowledge?" (Pause for an answer.) "This little booklet, the *Four Spiritual Laws*, will help you know for sure that you will go to heaven when you die."

If the answer is no, say:

"You can be sure that you are going to heaven. This little booklet, the *Four Spiritual Laws*, tells how to know."

God will show you other ways to introduce this material. The important thing is to keep your introduction brief and to the point.

---

[2] It is estimated that over 1.5 billion *Four Spiritual Laws* booklets have been printed and distributed in all major languages of the world.

Fasting & Prayer

In 1994, I felt led by God to undergo a 40-day fast. During that time, God impressed on me that He was going to send a great spiritual awakening to America, and that this revival would be preceded by a time of spiritual preparation through repentance, with a special emphasis on fasting and prayer. In 2 Chronicles 7:14, God gives us a promise of hope that involves repentance:

> If my people, who are called by my name, will humble themselves and pray and seek my face and turn from their wicked ways, then will I hear from heaven and will forgive their sin and will heal their land.

Fasting is the only spiritual discipline that meets all the conditions of 2 Chronicles 7:14. When a person fasts, he humbles himself; he has more time to pray; he has more time to seek God's face, and certainly he would turn from all known sin. One could read the Bible, pray, or witness for Christ without repenting of his sins. But one cannot enter into a genuine fast with a pure heart and pure motive and not meet the conditions of this passage.

Because of this promise, God has led me to pray that at least two million North Americans will fast and pray for forty days for an awakening in America and the fulfillment of the Great Commission. As millions of Christians rediscover the power of fasting as it relates to the holy life, prayer, and witnessing, they will come alive. Out of this great move of God's Spirit will come the revival for which we have all prayed so long, resulting in the fulfillment of the Great Commission.

I invite you to become one of the two million who will fast and pray for forty days. Also, I encourage you to attend the Fasting & Prayer gatherings held each year. If you feel God leading you to participate, please let us know on the Response Form. For more information, see the Resources or call (800) 888-FAST.

Other Resources by Bill Bright

Resources for Fasting and Prayer

The Coming Revival: America's Call to Fast, Pray, and "Seek God's Face." This inspiring yet honest book explains how the power of fasting and prayer by millions of God's people can usher in a mighty spiritual revival and lift His judgment on America. *The Coming Revival* can equip Christians, their churches, and our nation for the greatest spiritual awakening since the first century.

7 Basic Steps to Successful Fasting and Prayer. This handy booklet gives practical steps to undertaking and completing a fast, suggests a plan for prayer, and offers an easy-to-follow daily nutritional schedule.

Preparing for the Coming Revival: How to Lead a Successful Fasting and Prayer Gathering. In this easy-to-use handbook, the author presents step-by-step instructions on how to plan and conduct a fasting and prayer gathering in your church or community. The book also contains creative ideas for teaching group prayer and can be used for a small group or large gatherings.

The Transforming Power of Fasting and Prayer. This follow-up book to *The Coming Revival* includes stirring accounts of Christians who have participated in the fasting and prayer movement that is erupting across the country.

Resources for Group and Individual Study

Five Steps of Christian Growth. This five-lesson Bible study will help group members be sure that they are a Christian, learn what it means to grow as a Christian, experience the joy of God's love and forgiveness, and discover how to be

filled with the Holy Spirit. Leader's and Study Guides are available.

Five Steps to Sharing Your Faith. This Bible study is designed to help Christians develop a lifestyle of introducing others to Jesus Christ. With these step-by-step lessons, believers can learn how to share their faith with confidence through the power of the Holy Spirit. Leader's and Study Guides are available.

Five Steps to Knowing God's Will. This five-week Bible study includes detailed information on applying the Sound Mind Principle to discover God's will. Both new and more mature Christians will find clear instructions useful for every aspect of decision-making. Leader's and Study Guides are available.

Five Steps to Making Disciples. This effective Bible study can be used for one-on-one discipleship, leadership evangelism training in your church, or a neighborhood Bible study group. Participants will learn how to begin a Bible study to disciple new believers as well as more mature Christians. Leader's and Study Guides are available.

Ten Basic Steps Toward Christian Maturity. These time-tested Bible studies offer a simple way to understand the basics of the Christian faith and provide believers with a solid foundation for growth. The product of many years of extensive development, the studies have been used by thousands. Leader's and Study Guides are available.

Introduction: The Uniqueness of Jesus
Step 1: The Christian Adventure
Step 2: The Christian and the Abundant Life
Step 3: The Christian and the Holy Spirit
Step 4: The Christian and Prayer
Step 5: The Christian and the Bible
Step 6: The Christian and Obedience

Step 7: The Christian and Witnessing
Step 8: The Christian and Giving
Step 9: Exploring the Old Testament
Step 10: Exploring the New Testament

A Handbook for Christian Maturity. This book combines the *Ten Basic Steps* Study Guides in one handy volume. The lessons can be used for daily devotions or with groups of all sizes.

Ten Basic Steps Leader's Guide. This book contains teacher's helps for the entire *Ten Basic Steps* Bible Study series. The lessons include opening and closing prayers, objectives, discussion starters, and suggested answers to the questions.

Resources for Christian Growth

Transferable Concepts. This series of time-tested messages teaches the principles of abundant Christian life and ministry. These "back-to-the-basics" resources help Christians grow toward greater spiritual maturity and fulfillment and live victorious Christian lives. These messages, available in book format and on video or audio cassette, include:

How You Can Be Sure You Are a Christian
How You Can Experience God's Love and Forgiveness
How You Can Be Filled With the Spirit
How You Can Walk in the Spirit
How You Can Be a Fruitful Witness
How You Can Introduce Others to Christ
How You Can Help Fulfill the Great Commission
How You Can Love By Faith
How You Can Pray With Confidence
How You Can Experience the Adventure of Giving

A Man Without Equal. This book explores the unique birth, life, teachings, death, and resurrection of Jesus Christ

and shows how He continues to change the way we live and think today. Available in book and video formats.

Life Without Equal. This inspiring book shows how Christians can experience pardon, purpose, peace, and power for living the Christian life. The book also explains how to release Christ's resurrection power to help change the world.

Have You Made the Wonderful Discovery of the Spirit-Filled Life? This booklet shows how you can discover the reality of the Spirit-filled life and live in moment-by-moment dependence on God.

The Holy Spirit: Key to Supernatural Living. This booklet helps you enter into the Spirit-filled life and explains how you can experience power and victory.

Promises: A Daily Guide to Supernatural Living. These 365 devotionals will help you remain focused on God's great love and faithfulness by reading and meditating on His promises each day. You will find your faith growing as you get to know our God and Savior better.

Resources for Evangelism

Witnessing Without Fear. This best-selling, Gold Medallion book offers simple hands-on, step-by-step coaching on how to share your faith with confidence. The chapters give specific answers to questions people most often encounter in witnessing and provide a proven method for sharing your faith.

Reaching Your World Through Witnessing Without Fear. This six-session video provides the resources needed to sensitively share the gospel effectively. Each session begins with a captivating dramatic vignette to help viewers apply the training. Available in individual study and group packages.

Have You Heard of the Four Spiritual Laws? This booklet is one of the most effective evangelistic tools ever developed. It presents a clear explanation of the gospel of Jesus Christ, which helps you open a conversation easily and share your faith with confidence.

Would You Like to Know God Personally? Based on the *Four Spiritual Laws*, this booklet uses a friendly, conversational format to present four principles for establishing a personal relationship with God.

Jesus and the Intellectual. Drawing from the works of notable scholars who affirm their faith in Jesus Christ, this booklet shows that Christianity is based on irrefutable historic facts. Good for sharing with nonbelievers and new Christians.

A Great Adventure. Written as from one friend to another, this booklet explains how to know God personally and experience peace, joy, meaning, and fulfillment in life.

Resources by Vonette Bright

The Joy of Hospitality: Fun Ideas for Evangelistic Entertaining. Co-written with Barbara Ball, this practical book tells how to share your faith through hosting barbecues, coffees, holiday parties, and other events in your home.

The Joy of Hospitality Cookbook. Filled with uplifting Scriptures and quotations, this cookbook contains hundreds of delicious recipes, hospitality tips, sample menus, and family traditions that are sure to make your entertaining a memorable and eternal success. Co-written with Barbara Ball.

Beginning Your Journey of Joy. This adaptation of the *Four Spiritual Laws* speaks in the language of today's women and offers a slightly feminine approach to sharing God's love with your neighbors, friends, and family members.

These and other products from NewLife Publications are available from your favorite bookseller or by calling (800) 235-7255 (within U.S.) or (407) 826-2145 (outside U.S.).

BILL BRIGHT is founder and president of Campus Crusade for Christ International. Serving in 172 major countries representing 98 percent of the world's population, he and his dedicated team of more than 113,000 full-time staff, associate staff, and trained volunteers have introduced tens of millions of people to Jesus Christ, discipling millions to live Spirit-filled, fruitful lives of purpose and power for the glory of God.

Dr. Bright did graduate study at Princeton and Fuller Theological seminaries from 1946 to 1951. The recipient of many national and international awards, including five honorary doctorates, he is the author of numerous books and publications committed to helping fulfill the Great Commission. His special focus is *NewLife2000*, an international effort to help reach more than six billion people with the gospel of our Lord Jesus Christ by the year 2000.

Response Form

○ I have received Jesus Christ as my Savior and Lord as a result of reading this book.

○ I am a new Christian and want to know Christ better and experience the abundant Christian life.

○ I want to be one of the two million people who will join you in forty days of fasting and prayer for revival.

○ I have completed an extended or forty-day fast with prayer and am enclosing my written testimony to encourage and bless others.

○ Please send me *free* information on staff and ministry opportunities with Campus Crusade for Christ.

○ Please send me *free* information about other books, booklets, audio cassettes, and videos by Bill and Vonette Bright.

_____
NAME

_____
ADDRESS

_____
CITY   STATE   ZIP

_____
COUNTRY

Please check the appropriate box(es), clip, and mail this form in an envelope to:

> Dr. Bill Bright
> Campus Crusade for Christ
> 375 Highway 74 South, Suite A
> Peachtree City, GA 30269

You may also fax your response to (800) 514-7072, or send E-mail to newlifepubs@ccci.org. Visit our website at www.newlifepubs.com.

This and other fine products from NewLife Publications are available from your favorite bookseller or by calling (800) 235-7255 (within U.S.) or (407) 826-2145 (outside U.S.).